Hindsight 20/20

Hindsight 20/20

CARLOS HARLEAUX

Published by 7th Sign Publishing

peauxeticexpressions.com

Book Cover Design by Gibbs Hightower IV
Photography by Chris Booth

Copyright ©2013, 2020 by Carlos Harleaux

ISBN-13: 978-0-578-65283-2

Printed in the United States

Harleaux, Carlos
Hindsight 20/20—Second Edition

All rights reserved. No part of this book may be reproduced or transmitted in any form or by any means without written permission from the author/and or publisher.

Table of Contents

Hindsight Is 20/20 1
Appetizer 3
Just Give Me a Pen 5
Good Intentions 7
Rest Easy 9
A Fighter 11
Elephant in the Room 13
The Let Down That Won't Let Up 15
Holidaze 17
Fire Drill 19
Her Name Is Temptation 21
Leave Broken Glass Alone 23
Kissing Dirt for Now 25
Identity Theft 27
F.E.A.R. Factor 29
It's A Celebration 31
Popped Bottles 33
Back Burner 35
Cold Fingertips 37
Teeter Totter 39
Canvas 41
Lemonade 43
In Less Than 10 Minutes 45
Love In HD 47
Musical Chairs 49

Don't Talk to Strangers	51
Band Aid	53
First Mind	55
My One Regret	57
Vs Myself	59
Never Let Go	61
Quiet the N.O.I.S.E.	63
In Security	65
What the People Want	67
Numb Never Felt So Good	69
Rocks Get Tired Too	71
My Bleeding Heart	73
Standing On Your Shoulders	75
The Black Rose	77
SNL (Socially Neurotic Love)	79
Inside Your Mirror	81
Bulletproof	83
Just Words	85
Tongue Kiss of Life or Death	87
Tongue Twister	89
Throw in the Towel	91
Stagnant	93
Nice Guys	95
Praline Dreams	97
Sweet Lies	99
Celiwhat?	101
Bitter	103
Finish Line Poems	105
Beat Me	107
Jealous Hearts	109
Promises Unkept	111
Stampede	113
Fireworks in a Bottle	115
Commercial Break	117

Phantom	119
No Guarantees	121
Smooth It Over	123
Stay	125
I Remember	127
Changing Faces	129
No Second Chances	131
Save Me a Seat	133
I Am What I Was	135
Willing or Won't You	137
Mosh Pit	139
Leggo Your Ego	141
Seduction of the P Word	143
Check My Resume	145
Tattoo	147
Side Effects	149
I'll Never Tell	151
Get Off My Shoulder	153
Walk On	155
Forgo Forgiveness	157
The Power of the F Word	159
Don't Look Back	161
Lonely Two	163
Comfortable Silence	165
Detox	167
I Hope Your Roses Never Lose Their Bloom	169
Hindsight	171
A Swipe in the Wrong Direction	173

Hindsight Is 20/20

IMAGINE LIVING IN a world of just black and white. Not black and white in terms of race, but black and white in terms of our outlook on life. Many people do not like looking back in their lives, simply because they believe it holds them to the past. That can be true if we linger too long. However, in order to move forward, we must look back sometimes. It's a little bit like driving a car. At some point, you have to look in your rear-view mirror for a clearer view to help you reach your destination. When we refuse to look back, examine ourselves, admit our flaws and take responsibility for our actions, we diminish our real value. Who wants the dusty black and white TV with the old-fashioned turn knob? Not anyone I know.

So how do we transition from living in black and white to living in color? The first step is hindsight. Hindsight is simply the act of looking back. As the saying goes, looking back always paints a picture of perfect vision (hindsight is 20/20). It's the aha moment we always seem to miss when we're amid blurred vision. Then, the light switch comes on and we can see the 20/20 picture that hindsight had waiting for us all along. Our dreams, goals, relationships and interactions with people are in HD color and feel so close that it seems we're wearing 3D glasses.

Hindsight 20/20 will take you through the journey of many of the thoughts and feelings we have when we look back. There is forgiveness, bitterness, joy, and most of all understanding. Looking back isn't always a beautiful process. In the end, we're stronger, better and charged to move forward because of it. Let's go back for a moment, so we can have the most vibrant future we can ever imagine.....

Appetizer

I am not your cheddar biscuit
Cheese stick, fried green bean or
Tantalizing hot wing dipped in habanero sauce
I am not a left side of the menu option
Just to curb your hunger
Cleanse your palate
Or whet your appetite
Because I am the thirst quencher
And I will drown you
No teaser and preceding the 2ND, 3RD, 4TH and 5TH
Because I am the first.....and only
The main course, so have your to go box on stand by
I am your steak and potatoes, corn on the cob, black eyed peas
Pot full of greens, cornbread, peach cobbler and long island tea
It's like that?
Yes, it is, so heed the warning
And govern yourself accordingly
Because I am not your appetizer
Your finger food
Happy hour 5 to 7 special
Your left side of the menu option
Direct your gaze to the center of the page or
Look elsewhere
Either way I remain uncompromised
Because I am not your cheddar biscuit

Just Give Me a Pen

Give me a pen
So I can have written memory
Of love so good
I could not
Utter its existence
Give me a pen
So I can speak my mind's organized noise
Outkasting negative energy with a few strokes
Dotted i's and crossed t's
It's a moment to behold
So, throw me a pen
So, I can scribe upon a
Positive state of mind
Affirming only the achievable
That is fully attainable
So I can tell you how much
I hate you
Because you may not remember
What I said but
You can quote what I wrote
Just give me a pen
And not a pencil because
I will never be erased
But etched and sketched
In permanent time and space

Good Intentions

The soles of these good intentions
Were never built for walking
And my feet are cracked and calloused
Standing on their empty promises
The band aid to this massive gash
Is only a temporary fix
Elevation to only return to ground level
A momentary lift
I want to believe that what you say
Is married to your actions
But there is too much inconsistency
And unfaithfulness in your utterances
I've unstrapped the weight of my ego
Just in case that was weighing down
My judgment
But now I'm running naked
With nothing but these shoes and soles
Hole in my soul
And still left with only these good intentions
That never seem to progress into your best
And I just get bitter
As you say it will get better
And neither one of us can find rest
Or better yet our best
These good intentions are
Simply not good enough
To sustain me
When put to the test

Rest Easy

You have always been a fighter
Armed with courage, spontaneity and a
Lively personality that filled the room
With broad shoulders
You carried the load and
Whatever trials washed in with the tide
Because that's just who you were
You provided for your family
Without complaint and stood up for us
When we needed you most
Your love for us was genuine and true
Without a blemish
Because that's just the kind of man you were
We will miss you
Shed some tears
And laugh about fond memories
But, it's your turn to rest easy now
For all the times you ensured we could
Lay down your artillery
You have served us well and fine
These wounds will heal in due time
And you'll still be there
Watching over us
Like you were right there by our side
Because that's just the kind of man you always will be

A Fighter

"THAT BOY CAN call me whatever he wants to." To this day that is one of the fondest memories I have of my grandfather who passed away in 2019, Collins Kyle. When I was a baby, I couldn't pronounce his name correctly. I called him "Cowens" instead of "Collins". As I grew older, even after I knew how to say his name correctly, I never called him grandfather. I called him Collins.

He didn't seem to mind at all. In fact, if anyone questioned why I addressed him by his first name, he would quickly rebuttal their comment with the quote above. He was one of the most quick-witted men I've ever known. At times, he could be contrary too.... but that was part of what made him unique.

The last time I saw him was on Father's Day; it was a fitting send off. I didn't realize that would be my last time seeing him, but he was "fatherly" in every sense of the word. He was protective over his family, stood up for what he believed in, and didn't ever seem defeated by anything.

Collins was such a fighter that I remember thinking, *Wow, his only defeat was in death*. However, I was wrong. He wasn't defeated but he transcended to something greater. Now, I'm often reminded of him through the small things that creep up in my day to day life. I take it as his presence is still here and the legacy of his fight always brings a smile to my face.

Elephant in the Room

The must and huskiness
Of this issue reeks with stench and despair
Africana Loxodonta
This magnanimous beast has appeared
Out of nowhere
Can't climb above it
Can't tip toe around it
No ducking underneath it
Or hoping it won't find me
Lock, stock, and barrel
I am forced to stare at this mammal
Face to face
Faced with fate
The writing's etched on the wall
But my faith won't be erased
The Earth shudders beneath me
There is no escape or use
In calling for help
This test was designed specifically
For me, myself and I
Not somebody else

The Let Down That Won't Let Up

ONE OF THE most dangerous things we can do in life is place people on a pedestal. I have been placed on a pedestal by others and placed people on pedestals. The result is usually disappointment. People are human and always make mistakes. Yes, always.

At the end of 2019, I did some deep soul searching about some of my best achievements and lowest valleys. All the low points were primarily because I put too much trust in a person or situation. This is not to say we should live without expectation. Expectations are the fundamentals to solidifying standards that we all need to have.

However, we must be careful of expecting people to handle situations in the same manner that we would. Honestly, I'm still learning this one. Nevertheless, the more we place people up higher than they should be (above ground) we just set ourselves up for a major let down. Accept people for who they are and tailor your actions accordingly. Trust me, you'll save yourself plenty of confusion, frustration, and heartache in the long run.

Oh, wait. There's one more person we can't forget to take down from the pedestal – ourselves. Sometimes, we can be our own worst enemies by raising the bar to a level no one asked for us to meet. I'm guilty of this one. Plan properly and work towards your goals but leave room for others (and yourself) to make some mistakes along the way.

Holidaze

There'll be no opening fireworks
Without sparks to ignite from you
No candy-coated hearts
Or chocolate chunks to chew
I'd rather taste you
I'll be your April fool
From May to next March too
No matter what they say
I'll stay sticking by you
Life without you is just a
Rocky Horror Picture Show
So won't you come bring back
And be what I'm so thankful for
Because I'm in the dark
With no light to glow
Don't give me that mistletoe
Unless it's with you that
I'm nose to nose
Take these presents under the tree
All I need is you in a bow
To make my wish list complete
There'll be no closing fireworks to
Reflect and appreciate
It's just another one of those
Gloomy holidaze without you

Fire Drill

We were caught up
In our pleasure and pain
Masked by the sirens and
The thundering rain
I sighed, you followed
As we looked toward the window
Even if it's a real test
We'll wait until the smoke
Dusts the window
The flames are burning
Though not visible to the naked eye
Only ours
Lips locked; toes popped
Not a care against the wind
The smoke rolled under
The soles of our feet
As the flames danced against the door
Knocked to get inside to rival
The ones between us
So engulfed in each other
We were oblivious that
We sparked the very fire that surrounded us

Her Name Is Temptation

This beautiful temptress
Sings sweetly in the key
Of sultry seduction
She knows just what
Buttons to push to
Get me going
Leading me right to the edge
Just close enough to taste
Where hunger overtakes me
And replaces rationality's face
This love is justified, in my mind
That's all I need to get by
Nonsense to ever ask why
She prepares her thrown
Clad in deep, passionate hues
Camouflaged to the darkness
Watching every move
She's quite the voyeur
As she peers into
The peephole of your soul
Uninvited, and detests the light
Right before you can muster up a scream
You've just been tangled in the night

Leave Broken Glass Alone

There's blood on the floor
My eyes are filled with sweat
Furiously searching for a simple answer
Body is tired, muscles overstretched
With each step, it cuts a little deeper
With each grip, it burns a little further
Everybody says I'm a fool
But that just makes me climb a little higher
Elbows, shoulders, knees, toes
There's a scarred memory left to tell
Of what my mouth is too exhausted to say
The gutter offers no lower point than this
The shattered reflections of yesterday
Were once blinding with
Brilliance and radiance
Now everything falls dim and desolate
In the silence where the realization screams
That there's danger in piecing together
Broken dreams that were never
Meant to connect

Kissing Dirt for Now

I may be here now
Laying wearily with my nose
Kissing the dirt
Eyes closed to protect myself
From the elements
Fingernails digging through the ground
Trying to climb my way out
But this will not last for long
This is not my ending
It's just the beginning
Just the beginning
Of a new chapter
I may seem lost in direction to you
But I am merely finding my way back home
I am currently, but not permanently down
I am equipped to turn this situation around
I believe what will come into existence
So many times, we fail to realize
That our negative thinking is what gives
Our progress the most resistance
It's time to get up.....

Identity Theft

Who are you?
Under the clothes?
Under the lies?
Under the mask?
Beneath the disguise?
If your soul could be scanned
How much would you ring up to be?
Your bar code has been changed so many times
It would be difficult for anyone to see
Blaming others for your mental
Spiritual and physical bankruptcy
But no, it was you who overspent
On people, time, places and spaces
That only diminished your worth
This is not a case of stolen identity
This is the result of failure to
Tap into the remedy of a better
Me, she, he and we
No forced entry
Because the latch to the lock was unhitched
This is not a case of stolen identity
But one that is a reflection
Of your own worst enemy....yourself
So again, I ask....who are you?
Are you taking charge of your life
Or blaming it on being a victim of identity theft?

F.E.A.R. Factor

EVERYONE IS AFRAID of something. Children are afraid of the dark. Teenagers are afraid of acceptance and peer pressure. College students are afraid of the massive job force that awaits them and where they fit into it. Adults are afraid of so many things...failure, commitment, love, and even success. The funny thing is adults are the least likely to admit they are afraid of anything. Fear is a Catch 22 emotion. It can hinder your progression and propel you forward at the same time. The question is which direction will you allow fear to sway you?

A few months ago, I had the opportunity to hear actor/author Hill Harper speak at a company event for my job. I didn't expect much, but his speech was a pleasant surprise. The premise of his topic was fear and how we allow it to hold us back. One of his quotes that he stated has still stuck with me. He didn't coin this phrase, but it was very profound nonetheless (and it was my first time hearing it). "Fear is False Evidence Appearing Real".

Basically, what this means is that fear is nothing more than an illusion. We get so worked up behind the illusion, that we lose sight of the reality. Because of fear, we believe that we will fail. We will lose. We will die. We will be defeated. We will be left all alone. We will not succeed. And yes, all of these things are possible and can happen. But what about the flipside of fear that says we are victorious? We are loved. We are winners. We are blessed. We are worthy.

Failure is not the worst thing that can happen to us. It can actually be the beginning of something beautiful. So what if you fail? You learn, get up, try again or try something new if that doesn't work. We should never let fear hold us back, only push us forward.

It's A Celebration

The lights are flashing
Horns are blaring
Tight dresses and high heels
And the eyes are glaring
The mood is vibrant as
Confetti blankets the streets
Razor sharp edges
Perfume couldn't be sweeter
To me it stinks
How quickly we forget the bridge
That transported us safely
To the other side
How quickly we use wet handkerchiefs
As celebratory rags
Like a second line dance
Wonder what they were filled with
To begin with
How quickly we forget
Or did we ever really care???

Popped Bottles

I often wonder what the bottles think
As the celebration ensues
Vibrations from the bass thump and
Rattle the corks before they are even loosened
Before the overflow spills all over the floor
As everyone waits with their glass extended
Waiting for the lucky pour
Somehow, we think it's synonymous
With watching all the bad decisions,
Procrastination and uncomfortable hesitations
Swim off the surface
Leaving nothing but the cream of the crop
To pour in a vessel that holds our prosperity
The bottles tilt their heads back
Sitting right side up and cackling incredulously
"Yeah right," they say
"They'll be up to the same ole mess
Of tricks by this time next year"

Back Burner

Low...medium....hot.... I'm boiling
Danger on the stove
Smoke so thick
You can't control it
Careful creeping close
Be forewarned of combustion
You plus me
Equals your self-destruction
As the steam hits your skin
Closer than your next of kin
Separate you by the grain
Like my name was Uncle Ben
At best just a misfit,
General run of the mill Bisquick
Pancake, spatula
Flipped, it's over
Ruckus on the stove
Move it to the back burner

Cold Fingertips

What is this?
What are these foreign, frigid objects
That graze my skin?
This feels like déjà vu
Though I never knew I could feel
This confused with you
Who knew?
My mind runs questions
Longer than the Egyptian Nile
I smile and look at you
But you're not the same
Your touch is so cold
Leaving icicles in my veins
Not to mention that chilling sensation
That travels to my brain
Like a tingled touch tracing my spine
Yet this is quite different
This is quite frightening
The one I thought I knew is
Intertwined in this blizzard of emotion
My other senses give me
Reassurance along the way
But when you touch me, it's so cold
It becomes torrid
We grew so icy
Wouldn't you say?
Or is it too much of me to ask
For you to see it my way?

*Our hearts have turned frozen
Wouldn't you agree?
Your touch gets colder
As I get a numbing grasp on reality
You're not here with me
And I must defrost each time
At the most awkward moments
Your cold fingertips always find a way
To cross my mind*

Teeter Totter

Teeter totter
Feeder fodder
Suspended here in the balance
Between pride and humility
Your ringer was off
That's what you said last Tuesday
And the Wednesday before
And the Monday preceding that day
But I'm still here holding on to
What, I do not comprehend
I try to make your intentions malleable
With each bend, pull, and stretch
Yet to no avail
I'm still here on this teeter totter
Feeder fodder
Dangling in the breeze
Swaying between sensibility and sanity
You say things will change
But I see nothing but
A different shirt on your back
Yet I've remained the same
Too readily available and willing
At your mark, set, go
I know this is unhealthy
But I have grown so used to
This teeter totter
Feeder fodder
I know whose I am

But somehow, I've forgotten to
Wear that crown
So I'm here.....waiting
On your permission to be free

Canvas

Sometimes I look at you
And wonder if you know
The picture you've painted
On the canvas of my mind's eye
From fiery red flecks of passion
Anger and love so strong to hate
To blossoming blues
Of calming waves I use to splash
Like water on my face
Like the sunshine that rises
And sets when I think of you
To the nonchalant off whites
That intrigue with mysteries like the moon
So bright it hurts to look
Head on collisions with
The most powerful forces of
Beauty and its beast
Your purposeful tease of meaning
Sometimes I want to destroy it
And other times I want to embrace it
Yet I still look at you and wonder
If you really understand the labyrinth
Of the mystical masterpiece you've painted
On this canvas of my mind's eye

Lemonade

That cool, quenching, sensational tang...
I make haste to have these sweet juices
Dripping down my face,
Embracing the aftertaste,
Earthquake and aftershock of you
I am an intricate detail
In this simple amalgamation
But you are the catalyst to
Jump start the sparks of
These independently heightened fireworks
Dissipating with the bitterness
Of a lemon drop
On an unhealed wound
The salve of you
Citrus, miss this when you're away
This chilled refreshment
Is only concocted
Whenever you're in the mix
Summer bliss, sun kissed warmth
Glass sweats, grip gets looser
But we still hold on
Never letting go of this euphoria
And when the ice melts
I help the diluted taste
Of these sweet juices
Dripping down my face
By adding more of you

In Less Than 10 Minutes

A kiss on the neck
Breathing slow in my ear
Hands rubbing on my head
Fingers gripping your every strand
Unzip my dress and jeans
Slide down my Vickie's please
Throw my boxers in the corner
Get ready for the TKO
Heavy breathing and petting
Skipping the foreplay
And the condoms too
Just get straight to it
Rushing to get to emptiness
In less than 10 minutes
Telling me you love me
But you lie, you just love.....it
Don't get it confused
Reaching for mountain peaks
And fate's shadow is peaking through
In less than 10 minutes
The beast in me will be Unleashed in you
To become the itch in us
That we just can't scratch
Can somebody tell me how
All of this can happen
In less than 10 minutes?

Love In HD

Picture perfect
Visually appealing
Senses heightened past the ceiling
Something like 3D
But you can take your glasses off
Breathtaking clarity
You can reach out and touch
Witness this 1080p
Don't speak
I know what you're thinking
This Blu Ray is powered up and ready to go
Come get this love in HD

Musical Chairs

The music plays in the background
Sometimes softly, sometimes triumphantly
Sometimes emphatically and at times feels melancholy
Though the tune changes without warning
There's one thing I can count on
And that's the stopping of the beat
The echo of the trumpets
The last piano chord and guitar string strummed
Remnants of melodies fill an empty room
As we hurry to find our place
And not get shut out of the game
No time to recollect what just happened
Because it's time to get up and do it all over again
Sometimes the feeling lasts for days
Others for mere minutes
We are circling around the same chair
And eventually someone must lose
Though neither one wants to release their place
This amazing race is getting old
So, I'll just let you have the chair
While the music plays at your discretion

Don't Talk to Strangers

Don't talk to strangers
Be inside before the streetlights begin to flicker
Always say please and thank you
Speak your truth with vigor
Stand for something so
You don't fall flat on your face
But wait...what of heartbreak?
What of love turned rancid?
Be candid, but don't step on any toes
Stay professional and keep
What little couth you have left
Save some for mystery and don't
Let all the cats come
Clawing out of the bag
Pack light
Don't throw off your chakras
Hydrate, exfoliate, and mind your business
But again....what of heartbreak?
Who makes the rules?
Why are they so easily broken?
What ways are there to cope with
Curving the one who wants you
Only to get curved by
The one you can't live without?
When in doubt, don't talk to strangers
Play by all the rules
Wait your turn
Cutthroat your way to the top

The early bird gets the worm
Don't talk to strangers
Unless they can tell you
How to get over a broken heart

Band Aid

You cannot ignore what
You are not willing to fix
The raw meat of the issue
Lies strategically betwixt
Your temporary solutions
And your conscience
This conjunction is a conundrum
Much more complicated than a catch 22
Because that can easily be
Caught, conquered and split in 2
Unlike this crass bag of disaster
That leaves me flat on my ass
After deep thoughts cannot divide
Happy moments cannot subtract enough
To change what's on the other half
Of the equal sign
It's time to face what
Cannot be erased
We are soldiers strapped for war
Ironically marching in place
With patches over skin
Like quilted tapestry
Trying to heal wounds
Soul sunken deep
Band aids alone were never meant
To cure your issues
They just help block out extra debris...
For a little while

So, rip it off
Even if it comes with
A little skin
You'll do yourself more of a favor
Than that band aid ever did

First Mind

You ever do something you regret?
And you know you never should've done it?
You ever get a funny feeling?
But instead you follow your heart
and push it aside
I should've known
The first time we met
I should've known by
The way she walks
Should've listened a little closer to
The way she talks
But I ignored it
You ever get into some...
You don't know how you got into
You ever get stuck in a situation
But don't know how to get out
If I had followed my first mind
This wouldn't be happening
If I had followed my first mind
We never would have hooked up
If I had just listened to myself
I would have known to walk away
If I had waited awhile longer
I would have seen her true face before today
You ever get caught in some...?
Half the drama ain't even mine
I wouldn't be in this predicament
If I had followed my first mind

My One Regret

"A life is best lived without regrets"
Said some random wise man
I heeded his advice and
Followed that mantra
Despite handfuls of moments that
Never should have happened
Most times, always I can say
I've stood behind all my decisions with pride
Or at least able to stand tall without it
But one deep regret has haunted me
Through the years
One thing I would fix that would probably have
Dried their tears
Eased the vice grip on my fears
I would have stopped to really savor
The flavor of the moment
Really see the intricate details of the
Tapestry woven in the details
Instead I balled it up and
Threw it on top of the bed
Where the rest of the pile goes
When I can't deal with it
I would have taken the time to
Really smell the fragrant perfume of the roses
Andre 3000 tried to warn us they'd soon
Smell like boo boo
Boo hoo
No use in crying over spilled milk

We were never going to drink anyway
I would take the time to
Inhale the beauty of now
With all the gorgeous chaos it holds
These moments I'll never get back
I wish I would have held them tighter
Before they inevitably slipped from my grasp

Vs Myself

I had a stare down
With the man in the mirror today
He gazed intently
Without uttering a word
Finally, he spoke the still, small words
Welcome back
Felt great to hear like
I was the prodigal son who returned
He congratulated me on
Finding my way again
I asked him what would happen if
I get derailed again
Or failure swallows
My best intentions and dreams
That's when he returned a mischievous grin
As I looked on, perplexed
That's when his hand reached
Through the mirror and
Clamped my mouth shut
"Never speak poison on your dream
Or defeat on your soul"

Never Let Go

The tight grip you once had
Has now been loosed
Don't know when or how
But the fact remains the same
Drifting away and searching
To find my way back to you
You let me down and disappointed
Now I'm disjointed, disconnected
Unplugged and left reflecting
On what you did to me
Yeah that's what I'll call it
Cause it's easier to place blame
Not responsibility
You turned away when I needed you most
I begged for you to stay
But you insisted you had to go
Until the light came on
My ah-ha moment
Your hand was always there
I was the one that let go of it

Quiet the N.O.I.S.E.

I LOVE GOING to the movies. If it weren't for the expensive cost of movie tickets, I probably would go every weekend. No matter what movie or theater you're in, you will always see an ad or commercial to keep quiet during the movie. Life is a lot like being in a theater. There's action, drama, violence, romance, comedy and even horror. But we'll never understand life (or movies) if we don't quiet the N.O.I.S.E. When our minds aren't properly focused on the featured presentation before our eyes, we can misconstrue the plot and miss important aspects of the film.

One of the noisiest, self-destructive emotions we can ever display in life is insecurity. Insecurity is extremely dangerous for this very reason: Not Operating In Security is Exhausting. In a sense you can say insecurity = N.O.I.S.E. Do you really want to keep up all that ruckus in your life? The funny thing is people usually associate insecurity in romantic relationships only. But it goes so much further than that. Insecurity can keep you from reaching your dreams, supporting those around you and living your life to the fullest. Have you ever been guilty of being insecure? Don't all raise your hands at once. I know I have. Let's all remember to quiet that noise of insecurity so that we don't miss any important details in life.

In Security

Somebody please take these
Handcuffs off me
With urgency
It's an emergency
My bitterness, my lust
My analytical mistrust
Is what's got me traveling
Through this confusing intra-state of mind
A rebel against the limits of reciprocity
I don't really mean it
So you should understand me
Search within the core
That's where you'll find the best of me
Never mind the jagged edges along the way
Because the way to love is pain
As this metal begins to scrape against my veins
This ignorance ain't bliss
Because after several failed attempts
I'm that hopeless penny with not one
But two holes in it
You see I never really learned
That the way to love is gained
By none of the actions I exhibited
Uninhibited acts of jealousy on the left wrist
And premeditated malice on the right
If I could just get these handcuffs off me
Maybe I could teach myself to sleep at night
But because I didn't operate in security

By rationalizing events ever so insecurely
I failed to realize that surely
Love is never a sense of stable instability
The sirens are coming closer
Somebody call security

What the People Want

The people want me to be more proper like
So I so eloquently changed my diction
Not to mention my appearance
They say they want me to
Take off my glasses because it
Makes me look a bit too nerdy
They say I would look better with
The beard, rather than the goatee
Shave off my hair
Cause the bald look is more becoming of me
Now they are sick of me being proper
And think I should roughen up my edges
Add a gold tooth
Wear my pants around my ankles
The people say they want me to
Speak about sex, bitches, tricks, foes and hoes
Money and cars
You know how it goes,
The people say they don't want to think
Or read between any lines
The people barely want to read
Maybe that is a contributing factor to their demise
The people say I should be versatile
And change with the wind
So, the people talked and the people laughed
The people gathered near and far
To witness the debacle they created
Their formula to birth a star

The people vanished one by one
Over time and far between
The people left no traces of
Intelligent or innovative beings
I look to my left
Then I look to my right
Damn, glad I never listened to the people
If I did, I would never be able to sleep at night

Numb Never Felt So Good

If you feel the need to
You can needle prick my finger
Kick me in the knee
Throw daggers in my back
And roll over my feet
I could walk through
Fire and ice
And never feel the freezing blaze
The tingle of my nerve endings
Has elevated to the highest plane
And now reached a climax
Fizzled out
Hypersensitivity has given way to Unbalanced chemistry
This mystery is not worth cracking
So I will leave it unsolved
I could write the script on
What your next line will be So save it
I don't need your
Pathetic soliloquies It is under me
It has smothered me
It has surrounded me
And now it's free from me....YOU
After so long I've made myself numb
No longer succumbed
To your predictable cycle
There's no feeling left
I'm done and numb never felt so good

Rocks Get Tired Too

I come in many shapes, sizes, colors and textures
I am dependable, responsible
And allow you to lean on me
As the kindest gesture
You are heavy so take your rest here
You waver and wander
And leave just to return
No one seems to care about the rock's tears
You have saturated me with
Your troubles, doubts, fears
Some last only for a season
While some of us have been here for years
The signs are visible
As erosion sets in
And I am sent through the fire
To provide a sturdier bench of sorts
For you to sit your tired ass on....go figure
But what about the rock?
What about its issues?
Is that important to you?
Just running to spill your soul
Wading in your own misery pool
Filthy waters that you more than likely
Got your own self into
So maybe it's time to pick yourself up
Because rocks get tired too

My Bleeding Heart

My heart bleeds Ink to paper
So I share it now
Instead of later
Give a little bit more
Than in conversation
Read between the lines
And accept this invitation
To a place where
Everything is not always
Carefully spelled out
Lean to your own interpretations
Whenever in doubt
This cloud of thought
That hovers above me
Is what inspires me
Pulls and tugs me deeper
Into an abyss of creative wonder
What I speak is my own
Unless otherwise noted
So don't try to steal my thunder
Clap, snap your fingers, or sit intently
In concentration
If you like what you hear
That's just icing on the cake and
Cause for celebration
Though this emancipation of
My imagination is for me and me only
But I am not selfish

And that is why I share it now
Instead of later
My bleeding heart
From pen to paper

Standing On Your Shoulders

We stand on his shoulders
And lean against his back
He is always there when we need him
Multi-talented, so he wears many hats
His time is valuable
And he runs his business well
There is no need to brag or boast
Because his presence alone tells
The builder, provider, director and preacher
The doctor, lawyer, athlete and teacher
He leads by example where many are sure to follow
His road is not easy and where few have even traveled
He is your father, your brother, your mentor and friend
He is all these things and more
There to lend his helping hand
And expertise over and over again

The Black Rose

Sometimes we can't see
The forest for the trees
All these prickly thorns and tumble weeds
Dead center in the core
Of all of this mass confusion
Lies a bed
This bed is not for sleeping because
No rest can be gained here
But there is something beautiful that remains
On its tattered pillow
The black rose
The black rose that radiates
With dark beauty and mystery It is the sole imprint of
Storm weathering and triumph
It is victorious, yet delicate
It is vintage, yet futuristic
Screaming its life story into the winds
Without ever howling or whispering
A single breath
Pay attention
They are all around you
Never count the black rose out
It always finds a way
To pierce through the light

SNL (Socially Neurotic Love)

I just can't bring myself to speak it
So I resort to virtual stalking
Sulking when I realize you liked 3 photos
But haven't responded to my last 5 texts
Did I inspire that smile and
Sparkle in your eyes in your last story?
Just pick up the phone!
I see your green light is on
So maybe I'll just message you there
Maybe that's doing too much and
I'll just play it cool
I can't be the first to call
But messages aren't so invasive, right?
Yes, I'll go for it
Then, I'll be able to see your read receipt
Am I blocked now?
I can only see a limited view of your profile
The one you said was just a friend, Biz Markie
He liked 6 of your posts between 1:31 and 1:33
What's that all about?
Oh, wait – a new message
But it's not you
I'm not sweating you
I just want to be there to
Apply a cool compress when you get overheated
Do you even realize it's been 56 minutes
Since you've seen my last outcry for attention?
It's still unattended and unreplied

Your green light is still on
So I'm logging off for now
To avoid driving myself into a tizzy
My battery is at 11%
I need to find my charger quickly
Maybe I'll watch some reality TV
Apply a salve to my burning misery
I checked my Twitter, Facebook, Snapchat,
Instagram and What's App
No traces of your online presence
Other than that damned green light,
The likes and the story that's set to
Expire in 1 hour
I lay my head on the pillow
Exhausted from the whole ordeal
Check my voicemails
Since there's nothing better to do
Hmmm....a missed call from you
A voicemail you left 4 hours ago
Saying it's been a while since we've talked
You know, the kind with vocal chords
Not finger taps
You were yearning to hear my voice
I call you back, ashamedly

Inside Your Mirror

If I were your mirror
I would want you to carry me around
So you can take me out
Whenever we're too busy to see each other
I'd be there to tell you I liked the first outfit better
Tell you that you look
Beautiful when you first get out of bed
I would show you the way
I see you everyday
In a light with brilliance, intelligence, and elegance
And when you need to get away
I could pull you in with me where no one
Could find us, where we could be lost in love I would show
you that you would never
Have to worry if I'm still happy.....
Because your reflection would show
What's in my heart
I would stand by you in times of doubt, trouble and fear
Reflect rays of hope and understanding
I would show you how you've changed my life
And made me a better man
I would tell you that I'd never want to walk
The streets of life holding anyone else's hand...

Bulletproof

I was strapped up
And ready for your ammunition
No one else had been able
To permeate through this armor
And I never thought the first would be you
No matter how hard I try
To fight against this war inside
You shoot right through
This bulletproof vest every time
Searching for a flaw to
Make me believe it's not that serious
But I'm just fooling myself
Clearly, I've been wounded
I've been shot but please
Don't call the paramedics
You gave no warning
And my feet were planted to no avail
Guess I'm not so bulletproof
When it comes to you

Just Words

Positive affirmations will not
Permeate through the labyrinth
That entails these negative
Consonant and vowel sounds
Catch 22 is so-to-speak
Or press rewind
In your mind in silence
To soak it all in and think
I kick you, jujitsu
You stab me, retaliate
We are far beyond
A great debate
These bruises nobody sees
But our soul turns blue, purple, green
I lie and say that it's ok
But that compounds, just builds mounds
To eruption, confusion, I lose it
Now prove it
That your point is right
I don't care to hear
These words here are nothing clear
Just trudging through
This state of mud
End up right back
Where we started from
It's just words
But the pierce is fierce
Let's see what's left

When the smoke is clear
It's just words
More than Anita Baker
We apologize
Up from the larynx
Then out from my lips
These words, they keep us in more.....

Tongue Kiss of Life or Death

It is said that the tongue is the strongest muscle in the body. But the tongue is much stronger than just the physical sense. Sure, we use it to eat, speak and drink, but its effects are lasting. The words we say when using our tongue can cut deeply. How could a muscle that is so small in comparison to the rest of our body pack so much power? The answer is within us. It may start as a bad habit that is passed down through generations, until someone is stronger than the tongue and breaks the cycle. Some people grew up hearing nothing but "You're stupid. You're dumb. You'll never be anything in life." While some are able to roll these words off their backs like water, others are pierced and stung by these words that have a lasting effect. The question is, do we love ourselves (and the people around us) enough to recognize the evil in this and stop the cycle before it continues?

Then there's the circle of people we surround ourselves with. You can tell a lot about a person by the company they keep. It's no secret that positive people tend to attract positive people, just like negative people attract those that are negative. But what happens when you slip up and let someone in your world that plants seeds of doubt, fear and jealousy in your mind? Could they be just bringing out our natural character? Maybe so, but maybe not. Friends and associates are just like food. Whatever we feed ourselves will eventually manifest itself in an external and internal fashion. Are you full of trash or substance?

Ok, so you may be thinking, "What if I can't change my surroundings?" That's when you have to dig into yourself to turn that tongue kiss of death into one of life. I think we all can agree that we are often our own worst enemy. We speak defeat on ourselves sometimes before anyone else ever will. We become what we speak, without ever realizing it. A lot of people know that TLC is one of my favorite singing groups. A few years before Lisa "Left Eye" Lopes died, she made the statement in an interview, "Sometimes I just hope a car hits me or something and takes me out of this mess so it won't all be my fault." We all know her tragic ending. She was killed in a car accident over 10 years ago. Could this have possibly been a self-fulfilling prophecy? Maybe you're not making statements that are that drastic. But even telling ourselves things like, "I'll never be good enough for this job" or "I'm always broke" has a way of haunting us.

So what will you choose? The tongue kiss of life or death? It's not easy, but let's all make a conscious effort to be careful of the things we say to others and even to ourselves. This does not mean we should walk around with our feelings on our shoulders, but it does mean that we have a greater awareness of the power of the tongue. Use the strength of that muscle to build up, instead of tear down.

Proverbs 18:21 Words kill, words give life; they're either poison or fruit—you choose

Tongue Twister

The same tongue that's used
To tickle and taste, will tease
That heals, will bleed
Turmoil and greed
My speech is a seed
Sprouting love, growth, lust and mistrust
Germinating your psyche
With thoughts to ponder
Flowing with the fluidity of fresh water
All with the roof of my L
The breath in my I
The full-lipped bite of my F
And the effortless Ease of
The embrace that awakens the need to
Speak life instead of invisible daggers
No more confirmations of defeat
Or remnants of deceit
The victory will be
If it is up to me to speak

Throw in the Towel

I'm the real thing
And it shouldn't feel good
To pay less
Image may not be everything
But how could you settle for this
Low budget Squirt to obey your thirst
What I got will give you
That mmmmm good
Nighttime sniffling, sneezing weezing
Relief kinda feeling, without the hangover
And you're just the ringleader of a circus
Hungover the trapeze
Entertaining yourself
With good fun at best
Bet you can't find just One good reason
To dumb yourself down
And pour your best part
Of waking up down the drain
You can't get enough
No matter how you try to refrain
To keep thinking you can get the max
Of my flavor with cheap substitutes...
Now that is the true definition of insanity

Stagnant

Like a river sleeping
Beyond the hills
No emotion, no passion
No excitement or thrills
Laying peacefully minding its
Own repetitious business
No beginning to the ending
Until one night the wind blew
In the east direction
Just a little past 2:00
Stopped dead in its tracks
A taste of new life,
A feeling of fresh air Felt a new sense of self
A new sense of peace
Until something happened
That scratched against the exoskeleton
Now stagnant waters relinquish
Away from tumultuous tides
Beyond the mountains, beyond the hills
With no excitement, no passion
No emotion or thrills

Nice Guys

She gets a thrill every time
He grips her neck
Then kisses her shoulder
And tells her she's his best...ever
A bruise on the eye
Cuts across her lip
MAC in her back pocket
You could say she's well equipped
As the nice guy hangs in the balance
The sirens are squealing
As he holds her and promises
Once she regains consciousness
That he'll never do it again
Whispered lies echo
The raw reality of the tip toe life
Walking on eggshells
Scared it will cause a fight
The nice guy is hanging by a thread
Tears hit the tombstone
And talks of remembrance
Of what was in yesteryear
Concealer can't cover this
As the nice guy sits
No longer hanging, but cut from the string
Did he really finish last?
Or did she chase the wrong dream?

Praline Dreams

I once had praline dreams of love
Crusted with an ever-slight scorch of
Butter and brown sugar
I licked my lips to rescue the residue
Quickly running down the corners of my mouth
Creamy with a light airiness that
Propelled me high above the clouds
More than 31 flavors of euphoria
Now....well....yeah...you know
I caught that drip before it
Traveled down the side of the cone
We were too hot to ever keep cold
Before we melted, boiled, and dissipated
Evaporated, but let's get back to that memory
I can still savor the taste
If I close my eyes and squeeze tightly
To caramel drips, honey dipped kisses
Don't get something started with that bottom lip
Yep, I still remember
Now....well....yeah....you know
Those praline dreams taste like
Apple cider vinegar
And nobody likes the taste of that

Sweet Lies

I can whisper honey drenched lies
In your ear and let them drip
Down your cheek
Tell you all the sweet things
You yearn to hear
And disregard the sting
Of the light of truth
It's blinding, surprisingly
We'd rather feel ourselves
Through the darkness like vampires
Reveling in the twilight of the night
I can bite my tongue
Until it bleeds, just to hold back
What is already written all over my face
Wouldn't that be cool?
We'd rather drown under waves of illusion
Than walk on the breathtaking beauty of verity
Disparity is only gained while we beat around bushes
Misconception from the inception
Don't give me the empty fillers of sweet lies
That provide no nourishing vitality
Raise your hand if you really want the truth!

Celiwhat?

It's ok to be celibate...
But your nagging buzz is louder
Than a stadium filled with bees
It's ok to have mind over matter willpower
But it's not ok to parade around without
A towel right out of the shower
Prayed up and in the word
But your words are always
Daggers of hate
Eat what's on your plate
Before you upgrade to 5 course meals
If you want me to be
An upstanding gentleman
Maybe you should stand up a little too
Then it's really ok to be celibate
And not celiwhat

Bitter

That sour taste
That icky feeling
Burns you up inside
Something doesn't feel right
And everybody knows
You've had enough
And your true feelings
You can't hide
When you put up a show
Defensive, ready to throw bows
When life throws you Another lemon
And you feel nothing
Left is to be given
Snapping at people
Who really care for you
They don't know you anymore And neither do you
But something's got to give
The bitterness must cease
The acidic anger scorches
Until you have left, no peace

Finish Line Poems

Sometimes you don't need a lot of words to get a point across. These are called "Finish Line" poems. I named them that because I started them and left them for your interpretation to finish or leave them as is. What would you add to these?

Beat Me

If he can beat me rocking the chair
Then he can sit in it
No need to ask....
I already know the answer
His feet must be tired from standing

Jealous Hearts

To see you walking with braided hands
Will gain no attentive reactions from me
At least not any you'll get to see
What lies in the heart of jealousy

Promises Unkept

Vow to the death
The truth of a lie
Snaps and crackles flare
Disaster popping off is nearby
When the things we say
Are just things we say

Stampede

Won't you come back to
Stampede on my heart?
It's so unhealthy
But it hurts so good

Fireworks in a Bottle

Have you ever witnessed fireworks
Inside a bottle?
The calm before the storm
The flicker before the flames start sparking
Reaching higher heights and eventually
Bursting into the darkness
What a beautiful sight
But only in the environment of freedom
Fireworks in a bottle are merely
A light show impeded by fragments of broken glass
For the whole world to see
Wouldn't you like to gather round and
See just how long it takes
Before the last straw breaks?
And creates the first hairline fracture
Before the explosion
Like having convulsions
This is uncontrollable
And cannot be contained
These fireworks are popping and
Growing with intensity
Lights shining brightly for all to see
Am I the only one who sees this entropy?

Commercial Break

White noise fills the background
As I channel surf for escapism
That's when I found you
A break from monotony
My temporary sanity
Most people push you away
To get back to their
Regularly scheduled program
But I welcome you with open arms
And could care less about this show
Everyone wants to see but me
Commercial break, you are
A breath of fresh air
As I sit in this rocking chair
Popcorn in hand
Remote on the table
I've been transported and dropped off
In a 3-dimensional sensation of a land
Then, zap....zooming in on bright lights
The studio audience is cheering
The show is back on
And I say goodbye to the commercial break
Until the next time

Phantom

This desire is thick
Unable to slice it with a knife
But so is the absence of your presence
In the moment
I wonder how this could ever be
Then poof…..the disappearing acts begin
MIA without an explanation
Perhaps is not my right to receive
I wonder how this game would end
If I reciprocated with the same disturbing behavior
Caught in the web of demands
Your unspoken communication screams
In lieu of words, actions and mentions
To be continued and yet to be confirmed
Decadent fruits taste sweeter when left unattended
Possibly that's your theory
Perhaps you prefer to build an uneven ground
Or not at all
Am I supposed to remain suspended in your web
Anticipating the break created from inconsistencies?
I'm all in for now
I'm invested though I know
My mind's eye suggests differently
I am here
Until I decide to vanish in the night
Just like you

No Guarantees

No matter how hard
We try to hold on
There are no guarantees
Tomorrow you may awaken
And find yourself out of love with me
Today she may realize that
Beauty is fleeting
And that's all that ever was
Next week he may realize
That sorry isn't enough
When the opportunity to apologize
Is no longer an option
We move in robotic motion Day in and day out
Depending on the clouds to
Shield the storms of life
And often times they do
But what happens when the
Rain cracks the sky
And the sun gives way to darkness Will we survive?
I took for granted all the things
That appeared to be so stationary
That crutch of a wall
I heavily leaned on
And now the sheet rock is breaking
In a life filled with hollow guarantees
Who is still left standing
When trouble shakes our dreams?

Smooth It Over

When the yelling stops
And the walls are left speaking
We are left barely standing
Our equilibrium still spinning
Desperately trying to
Reach for the rewind button
To go back to the future
We predicted
Happiness in HD
Maybe that's where we went wrong
Happiness fleets, joy stays
Going through the motions
Drudging through the pain
Unable to see the sky for the rain
No rabbit's foot or 4-leaf clovers can
Save us now
Have we become too rocky
To smooth over?

Stay

You know I want you to stay
But when I look in your eyes
I see the tears I've made you cry
Even when you're smiling
I feel the somber undertones
The unspoken resentment and
Unanswered questions
That's not a way to live
Or merely coexist
We persist in the push and pull
A tug of war of sorts, yet
We both give way and collapse
Into the muddy, uneven foundation
Beneath our feet
You know I want you to stay
But this kind of living doesn't
Seem like your forte
The Feng shui of our souls is interrupted
Just give me a place of zen
A sign to make the hard decision
That's never easy to say
You know I want you to stay
But your peace is priceless
Even if us is the cost to let you fly away

I Remember

I remember the texture of your voice
And the way I felt hearing it
Can't forget your smile
That still echoes off these walls
The way you walked into the room
And walked out of the door
I can still see it in the rearview mirror
I remember your perfume
So sweet I can still taste you
You've made it hard to move on
And do what must be done
There are so many memories of you
That flood my mind
That I sometimes can't help
But wade in this
Distant reality of mine
I remember so much and
That's my dilemma for sure
Sometimes I wish I didn't remember
Maybe that would be the cure

Changing Faces

My mind knows the truth
That my heart never lets go of
Breezing past consciousness
I can't seem to grasp hold of
What's the use in changing faces
When yours is all I see?
There's no need for replacements
If I can't have you
Get these faces out of my space
Because they do nothing but irritate me
Finding my way back to you
Through this labyrinth and masquerade
False pretenders
Lame contenders
No one comes close or
Even gets on my nerves
In that awesome way you do
No accolades are worth sharing
If they can't be won with you
You'd think with this revolving door
Of candidates, I'd have found a
Perfect match by now
But they are merely fractions of
Perfect imperfections
That I don't care to entertain
I'd do away with all the changing faces
Just to hold yours once again

No Second Chances

We keep it moving forward
Around these parts
No backwards steps
Or getting close enough to
Pull the strings of this heart
There was a time when
We would have stopped
To hear your side
Tried to stay to make things right
But those times have passed
Yes, it's nice to see you
I remember the fragrance of
That sweet perfume,,,,,and you
But the memories of
Bitterness and confusion
Still linger too
Some may call it cynical
But we call it protecting my heart
These feet were made for walking
With their share of stumbled steps
It's true
These feet just weren't made for
Running back to you

Save Me a Seat

Save me a seat
So I can see the clouds collapse
And crash on the concrete
Save me a seat
So I can smell
The sweet aroma of sorrow, victory
And the sweat of triumph
Make room for me and my bags
Of judgment, ridicule and
Hopelessness, restlessness,
Looking for someone to take this bait
And eat this poisonous nectar like us
And witness this isn't just us Injustice
But that's just it
A mirror of the mockery just shows
The joke's on us
Let me sit on your soul
To suffocate the screaming silence
Of my own poor existence
Save you a seat?
Someone will be more than happy to
You just can't sit next to me

I Am What I Was

Some say that it's good
To look back and say
I'm better than I used to be
But I am what I was
And I have not crossed over to
Used to be yet
Dogs chasing my heels give me
Insecure momentum
They always bark
But no bite like Bart's
Throw the darts aimlessly
Striking edges in the night
Might get mighty close
But never hit the bull's eye
We try to say goodbye
But choke up like Macy Gray
Caught up in the back street
But we don't want it that way
I am what I was
And that's the honest truth
If you can't grow from the past
Then what good are your roots?
I am what I was in past and
Present tense
This cycle is not logical
But makes perfectly insane sense

Willing or Won't You

You tell me you're here
Not under duress
I find myself being extra careful
Not to probe and press to
Reveal your true intentions
So I just settle for your words
In the meantime
Though I wish your actions would
Stick to them like marshmallows on smores
So sticky and malleable
Not easily separated
Melanin skin tones intertwined
Under the naturally dim orange lights
The physical vibration takes us higher
But I begin to descend
Once my feet leave the bed
If this is all we'll be
Just tell me so I can tame
My throbbing heart accordingly
Hmmmm.....sounds familiar
Sounds like all the things you used to tell me
Are you here or are you really here?
Really, I need to know

Mosh Pit

Will you be my mosh pit?
When I've become too inebriated
With the troubles of life?
Can I free fall to you
With unfailing support?
Or should I just keep performing
The same song and dance
Until the curtain call?
Something tells me
You may not be strong enough
To catch me
Not that I feel the need to
Fall back but it just
Feels good to know
There's a safety net nearby
So can you be my mosh pit?
Arms outstretched and ready
To catch my faults with my perks
Something's telling me it
Could all be in my head
And you've been there
Waiting all along
Something tells me you
Could be my mosh pit
But maybe I'm just afraid to fall

Leggo Your Ego

Sometimes I wish you could just pop
The toaster and loosen your grip
Unloose those screws that
Have got you locked
Dead bolted in your ways
That pride will soon go sour and
We would be much better off
If you could ever learn
To leggo your ego
Sticky syrup sweet
There's no room left in the seat for you
Cause you won't leggo
That frostbitten ego
Stale and beyond the sale by date
But I've got an ego too
One that's telling me
I should leggo you
Pick up me
This ego's done and bittersweet

Seduction of the P Word

It has been known to seduce. It has been known to divide. It comforts and heals. It conquers all feelings of honesty and creates jealousy. It kills and then blames you for the act. It eats away at your soul and lies at the root of all vanity....and disaster. It's the subtle warning before you see the flashing lights coming towards you. You won't see it on my sleeve. You won't always see it on their face. What is this dangerous P word? PRIDE!

I've been thinking lately about how pride hinders us (including myself) in so many ways. It tarnishes our relationships, friendships, and even our health. What is it about pride that is so attractive that we must hold on to it for dear life? I know I have been guilty of this before. Whether it's trying to be my own man when I'm sick (I prefer to just be left alone when I don't feel well) or being ashamed to admit that an unexpected expense causes me to need extra cash, I've done it. Don't you find it strange that even after we think we've learned the lessons from those prideful moments, we still fall into the same traps?

We exhibit at least one (if not multiple forms) of pride every day. Let's start with getting your clothes ready for work. Do you pick out that certain outfit on the meeting day with your big execs because you don't care how you look (probably not good, LOL)? Do you genuinely want to look your best, or do you want to impress those execs? Chances are, your answer is one of or a mix of the last two choices.

Then let's take that dream car you can't keep your eyes off. Is it a Bentley, Lexus, Maserati, or Mercedes? You may genuinely like these cars and if so that's how it should be. But how much do the desires behind our dream cars and houses really cater to what other people think, leaving what we want in the dark? Suppose someone's dream car is a Kia (I know.... highly unlikely). They probably wouldn't admit this too much, because it's not a status symbol vehicle.

Don't get me wrong, we should take enough pride in ourselves to look presentable, be confident, and know our own self-worth. Just like there's a thin line between love and hate, there's probably an even finer line between unhealthy and healthy pride (if there is such a thing). Just like some of the foods we eat, we have to use pride sparingly, because it's never good to be too prideful. No matter who you are, you will need forgiveness, a helping hand, or understanding at some point in your life. If it

hasn't happened to you yet, your turn is coming.

What are your thoughts on pride? Should we only possess a little of it or avoid this "P" word altogether?

Check My Resume

I am not impressed
By your plaques on the wall
Like Humpty Dumpty
They will eventually teeter totter
Topple over and have a great fall
I am not enthused
By your keyless entry
It will one day trip up
And you will lock yourself
Out of your own existence
Like the burglar bars
I have up for you mentally
I am not enthralled
By your pocket roll of cash
Sure, it spends but not on me
And without anything saved
It surely won't last
I am not amused by
Your technical gadgets
I am not interested in
Your intellectual stabbing
Condescendingly bending
Your viewpoints
On deaf ears
You do not matter to me
You who only thinks selfishly
You who only looks good on paper
And that's even relative

Do yourself a favor and
See how change
Tastes now instead of later
And don't spend all your life being a
Shallow paper chaser

Tattoo

Pictures, popularity, and clothes
They all eventually fade
But your impression has lasted
Tattooed on my brain
Etched in memories
That can't be erased
Food for thought to digest
Still room left on my plate
I breathe in to
Inhale each moment
And dread its release
In more ways than one
You have brought
To my life, an increase
Crossroads connect for
What seems like seconds
No need for timers
Or Microsoft Outlook reminders
Cause this right here is epic
So much so that
I'm watching myself reach out
To only collide with
A glass barrier
So near, yet so distant
But whatever the case
This tattoo remains
When all else fades
You are left engraved in my brain

Side Effects

Warning!
This drug may cause nausea,
Sleepless nights, euphoria, irritation,
Slurred speech
Blurred vision, dizziness, grand
Delusions, mass confusion
Puffy eyes, swollen glands and
Heart palpitations
Whether lethal injection or
Encapsulated ingestion
You are instantly released
In my blood stream
Unlike your typical
Over-the-counter medicine
This has no expiration date
On the brink of overdose
Wish I had read the warning labels
Plastered so boldly on the packaging
It's damaging, but there has been
No recall
Because everybody can't get enough
Pushing rationality aside
For a mere imitation
Who cares about the side effects
When you're getting
Instant gratification?

I'll Never Tell

They can tie me down
With barbed wire ropes
Beat me bruised, black and blue
In hopes that I'll utter a clue
Try again
They won't get me to betray you
They can entice me with the
Most titillating sensations my senses
Have ever know
But it will all be in vain because
Your secret is safe with me
I tried to tell them they
Don't have the strength to break
I tried to show them my loyalty
Is stable and unwavering
Yet, they test me
Still they pull out all their stops
To try to make a liar out of me
I laugh at their ignorance
As the pain reaches a point of
Numb familiarity
I wouldn't give you away for charity
Or any donation or
Inflated monetary exploitation
With patience, they think
My walls will crumble
Brick by brick
They only reach higher heights

I'll press my lips, bite my tongue and
Clench my teeth ever so tightly
I'll never tell, I'll never show
I'll be the sacred keeper of your secrets
And never let them go

Get Off My Shoulder

Taking off my shirt
And you can take these tissues Wringing myself dry
Of your oversaturated issues
Turning down these bright lights
That only glimmer and beam on you
Neglecting others and serving
Your narcissistic point of view
Turning off my phone
So, I can't hear the echoes
Of your vocalized ailments
It must not be so bad
If you went this long without
Taking care of it
You can turn your pillow
Until your tears saturate
Through the cotton
But I've gotten drenched
And I have nothing left to dry
Here but myself
So, you can get off my shoulder
And go cry to somebody else

Walk On

I will not try to chain down
What wrestles to be loosed
I will not coagulate this union
When one half yearns to be segregated
I don't have the genetic makeup or the
energy I will not smash the gas
If you insist on pumping the breaks
I cannot piece together good intentions
With so many missing pieces
I will not make excuses for the
Reality residue beneath you
Because I've got my own too
I will not compensate for
Imbalanced blame, lies and control
Never pull the trigger
On a gun you're scared to hold
Load your ammunition
And empty all your clips
You've become so predictable
In this game
That I'm more than well equipped
To withstand the bullets
Your possibilities are wide open
Just like the door
And if you feel the need to exit
Then all I can say is walk on

Forgo Forgiveness

I'm going to forgo forgiving you
It takes too much energy to smile and
Fake and laugh in your face
And take a deep breath...
When I really want to punch you
Like the poster child of
Every blood boiling moment
I've ever had rolled into one...fist
Make that two
When I think of you
I'm forgoing forgiving you
My stomach churns just to look at you
And the sweetest medicine
Is watching you suffer
Oh, don't look at me and
Point your fingers
Many of you bathe in this same acid
The ph balance of your soul is
Off kilter
So, when you cleanse your self
And make it out unscathed
Then come tell your truth
Until then I'll forgo forgiving you too
Oblivious to the fact that
You've moved on
While I'm still stuck here
Holding on to jagged
Crusty edges of memories

That only pierce my existence
Until I resemble a honeycomb
Holy, but not full of praise
You are worthy and I am out of place
Out of touch with reality
And missing the clear picture
Forgiveness ain't all about the listener
We must not forgo the element
That pertains to the speaker

The Power of the F Word

I'VE HATED. WON. Lost. Been on the receiving and giving end of second chances. Held grudges. Cut people off. Caused myself physical harm. Misunderstood. Loved. Gotten into arguments. Yelled. Made a fool of myself. Sat back and laughed as others have made a fool of themselves trying to get a reaction out of me.... all because of the F word....

Yep, I have done all of these things and more because of a simple word we all know.... Forgiveness. We all know it is right to forgive. It is therapeutic to forgive. It is beneficial to forgive. But is it ever easy to forgive? In some instances, yes, but most times NO! When we're in the heat of the moment of anger, hurt or pain, forgiveness is the last thing we think about. Sometimes, even if we do forgive quickly, we want to hold on to the anger just a little bit longer, so we don't look weak to the other person...crazy, isn't it? Sad to say, but it's true. Think about the last time you were angry at someone, and then think about how long it took for you to forgive them, or vice versa. Chances are there was a time gap there that shouldn't have been there.

I realized I was holding on to something that happened months ago, and the feelings had resurfaced. I wanted to capture that raw emotion we feel when we become upset. This is the time when forgiveness is on the back burner and retaliation is at the forefront. At this point there's almost no use in talking someone into a forgiving mindset, because they're probably not thinking straight....and you'll just end up getting hurt or upset in the process (sometimes it's best to leave broken glass on the floor...). Who do you need to forgive today? What are you holding on to because you never got that apology you thought you deserved?

Has everyone else forgiven you and you're the only one left to forgive? Sometimes we can be our own worst enemy.

Seek forgiveness, whatever the case may be.... even if it's from you. And if you don't get the forgiveness or apology you desire? It's not the end of the world. Just live in the way you want to be treated. Living in a state of bitterness primarily hurts you and not who you're mad at. Forgive and LET GO.

Don't Look Back

I'd rather never see
Your face again
Than to see you
Come back with that
Same look on your face
That same tone in your voice
And a story so familiar
I can finish your sentences
I was dreaming and so glad
Somebody woke me
Cause I can't live contently
In this state of chaos anymore
So, this time I won't beg you
I won't ask you why
Cause I already know
And I could care less to
Hear any more lies
If you decide to leave
Find the compass in the sky
That leads you far away from me
Don't look back
Don't turn around
If you're just going to come back
The same way you left

Lonely Two

Made a reservation
In a cozy little corner
Dim lights
Table setting for two
My mind's running marathons
We're not really here
Shift my energy
To be here with you
Present in a room full of strangers
In the company of likeminded people
We all are lonely hearts in a sea
Of miscommunication
Misguided intentions and
Off the beaten path with trepidation
"How was your day?"
"Fine, and yours?"
"What did you have for lunch?"
"A small salad and a side of chili...
But I wanted something more"
Double entendres fill the room
And create a space where
Unspoken expressions force
Meanings that drive the steak
Through our hearts with melted butter
Is it cooked to your liking
I used the napkin in my lap to
Wiped off the residue of our
Last savory crumbs

You placed yours in your lap
Lipstick left on the rim of the glass
As evidence
That we were there physically
Yet mentally in outer space
Don't find yourself making
These types of reservations
Because the worst kind of loneliness
Is to be tethered to withered love

Comfortable Silence

We both stare intently, not at each other
Directly ahead at the TV screen
We both laugh and sigh at different moments
That inspire an audible reaction from us individually
Closely we sit, peaceful and unbothered
In a room just cold enough to require a
Thin piece of fabric to knock the chill off
Our bare legs as we reach into the bag
For more chips
I let you have the last few whole pieces
Because you are worth much more than
Mere crumb snatching
Others may look at us and think
We are quite mismatched
Yet we snicker at their opinions
Knowing we are quite relaxed
Virtually attached at the hip
Saving the taste of cherry limeade and each other
Every time we lick our lips
We have not uttered a word
For over 3 hours and counting
Yet this euphoric feeling is priceless
Secluded in our own world
Of enjoying each other's company
Comfortably silent
No need to speak
Because I know just what you're thinking
This time, it doesn't hurt

Detox

You have poured acid
On my soul
Eating through
My faith and beliefs
I am hollow
And feel so cold
How did I get here?
To this delusional destination
I am short of breath and energy
In need of resuscitation
Relaxation, maybe take a long walk
Talk it, say it, shout it, yell it
Out of my system
So, I can get back to peace
Reclaim the me I know to be
Treaded lightly long enough
But I cannot wallow
In your toxic chemicals
Time to snatch my victory
This sour bitterness is killing me
I will not be a casualty
You have no authority

I Hope Your Roses Never Lose Their Bloom

Today their head's upright and
Tilted toward the sun
Arms open wide to receive
All we've become
Forgiving of our shortcomings and flaws
Remove the mask
Because the petals see it all
Beneath the sun's rays that kiss your neck
More ravishing and radiant than the day before
Careful not to disrupt the blinding splendor
I touch but I'm afraid to get too close
Promises were often made to be broken
But can you keep this one thing tried and true?
Promise your roses will never lose their bloom....for me

Hindsight

Some people say there's no good
In looking in the rearview mirror
But in this case, I can't help but
Look back and see things clearer
To a past that's now far
Removed from my mind
I was walking on
Black and white streets
But now I see in color
Radiant, vibrant and full of life
Those things that used to rack my brain
Are no longer areas of concern
For me to maintain
So, I thank you all for the
Lessons learned
And value gained
Everything was a blur
Because I was caught in
The middle of a whirlwind
But now I'm out of
The eye of the storm
And able to see the sun for what it is
I'm shining brightly
Blinding and scorching negativity Useless bickering
You're right and I'm wrong
I'll give you that and move around
Because I'm elevated to a level
That's far above this ground

HINDSIGHT 20/20

Looking back suddenly
Doesn't seem so bad

A Swipe in the Wrong Direction

A New Novella by
CARLOS HARLEAUX
Coming Fall 2020

"Candy? Hey, you finally answered this time. I've been trying to get in contact with you for a while. Um, how have you been?" Mike asked.

"The hostility just doesn't let up. I'm doing better. How are you? I'm sorry for being so MIA. I just had to take some time to get myself together. I was headed down a bad road," Cookie explained. Despite a few touch-and-go check ins, Cookie hadn't had in depth conversation with Mike in nearly a year.

Mike knew that she was still getting over Ken's death and didn't want to push her. He knew she needed to heal and grieve in her own time.

"It's ok, I'm honestly giving you a hard time. I'm glad to hear from you. How has everything been going on your end?" he asked.

"Oh you know, just looking after Breanna and trying to get myself together. Mike, I owe you an apology," Cookie paused.

"Ok, I don't think you do. For what?" he inquired.

"Yes, let me explain. I know a couple years ago I told you I was going away for a little while to regroup. That was a lie. I had become an alcoholic, Mike. You didn't deserve to be around me like that, even as a friend," Cookie continued.

Even as a friend? Mike thought. Did she mean that she was originally thinking that they could be more than friends? He didn't interrupt and let her finish her statement, without reading too far between the lines.

"I'm so embarrassed. I can't believe I just told you that, but I had to get it off my chest. We have really been through a lot," she exhaled.

"Cookie, don't you feel embarrassed for one bit. I'm very proud of you. I had no idea all that was going on. Regardless, you've done something not many women or people period have the courage to do. You're still an amazing woman and a wonderful mother. Don't ever doubt that," Mike reassured her.

He felt a pang in his heart. The thought of Cookie going through such an ordeal made him feel sick. Mike only wanted great things for her and wanted her streak of unfortunate events to finally be over; surely, she did as well.

"Mike, you have not changed after all these years. Why can't all men be like you? You are so loyal. Enough of my sad sap stories. Things are looking up for me now. God has spared me for some reason, so I have to give Him thanks and show that I'm grateful for another chance," Cookie stated.

"That's great to hear. God has really smiled on you, Candy. I wouldn't exactly say all men should be like me, but I appreciate the vote of confidence," Mike chuckled.

"Hey, I'm just saying. These guys out here are pathetic. I was trying to get back out there on the dating scene, but it's all been too much. So many of these men are losers. I know the ladies are all over you. Any new dating escapades on your end?" Cookie inquired.

Mike wasn't sure of her tone. She didn't seem to be asking for her own personal interest, but from the perspective of a concerned friend. She was a wild card though, so he could never be too sure of her intentions.

"My dating life is pretty lame. Work has been keeping me ridiculously busy," he replied.

"Come on now. All work and no play will drive anyone crazy," she interrupted.

"I'm serious. None of these women out here are really worth investing my time in," he concluded.

"Well, I understand that. Maybe you should try one of those online dating apps. I haven't had success with it, but I'm sure it's probably different for men. Everyone has a representative and it's all peaches and cream until their true colors start showing," she sighed.

"Online dating? Wait. You've tried that? I never would have thought in a million years that you would try online dating," he laughed.

"I know, right. I did and it was a disaster. It was one of those things I can check off the list and say I've done it. Been there, got the t-shirt, and only use it to work out in," she snickered. Mike responded with a guttural laugh.

"I can't say I'll be joining you on the online dating journey. Some of my friends have been asking me to try it. Hell, even my mom has. She thinks it's been way too long since I've had a serious relationship. You'd think it wouldn't be this hard to pick em in your mid-thirties, right?" Mike replied.

"Exactly. What are we gonna do?" Cookie laughed.

Mike felt a lump form in his throat. Everyone thought he wasn't dating because he was still heartbroken about his divorce. However, that wasn't the case. He was in love with Cookie, even after all these years. Maybe it was his chance to try again. His feelings for her were relentless and he didn't want to give up on the one woman he truly loved.

"Hey, you know....I've been thinking. I know you're working through some things. I'm working through some things. What do you say I take you and Breanna out for some ice cream this weekend?" he asked. Mike felt like a weight of bricks had finally been lifted from his shoulders.

"Mike, that sounds awesome. Let's play it by ear. I'm just so careful now. I mean, of course I know you, but I just need to watch out for Breanna's best interest. Plus, I don't know if I'm fully ready to get back out there and seriously date anyone. You are so sweet though," Cookie let him down gently.

"No worries. You can't blame a man for trying, right?" Mike replied nonchalantly.

Mike knew that "let's play it by ear" was Cookie's nice way of saying, "It's not gonna happen".

He was tired of waiting for her to see his value. There was only one thing left to do now. Mike decided he would just have meaningless, random sex with multiple women. There would be no strings attached and he would live in the moment.

www.ingramcontent.com/pod-product-compliance
Lightning Source LLC
Chambersburg PA
CBHW071359290426
44108CB00014B/1609